Starlight, Then and Now

Poems

By

Jessica Harman

Copyright 2013

By Jessica Harman

ISBN: 978-1-304-51121-8

The poems in this book may be reproduced

And shared in any medium as long as credit is given to the author, Jessica Harman.

Artwork and cover art and design by Jessica Harman

Are copyright Jessica Harman 2013

Published in the United States of America

Starlight, Then and Now

To Misha,

Happy Birthday,

with love

Contents

Book I: The End of the Rose   15

Symbiosis	17
Almost Finished	19
Necklace	20
Made of Light	22
Winter Music and Musing on Summer in L.A.	23
Superstar	24
End	25
Loss and Resurrection	26
Wound	27
Wings	28
Walking on Clouds	29
Sun	31
Nothing	33

My Taste in Men	34
Remembering the Dawns of Yesteryear, Waking up Today at 10:36 A.M.	35
Dawn	36
January Sun	37
Limbs	38
Light	39
Wheel	41
Lares and Penates	42
The Sun Is Going Down	43
There Is No Going Back	44
Blue Fire	46
The Fire Tree	47
Self-Deception	48
Baguette	50
The Clothes We Wore	51
Hands	52

Each Other	54
You	56
Rapture	57
Earth	58
For You	59
A Short Poem about Being Here	60
Lion	61
Rain	62

Book II: Time Went on and the Future Passed Judgment — **63**

For Julia	65
Patricia	67
Arnold	69
Act I	71
The One	72
One	74

Face the Music, Bitch	75

Book III

Subito Cogito, Ergo Sum   **77**

Shine	79
Corona	82
No	84
Heartbeat	85
Morning	86
Working a Day Job in Boston, Massachusetts	88
Café Café	91
Silencia	94
Daddy	95
Hole in One	96
Being Denim the Color of	
the Sky—Say What?!	98

Soggy Cornflake Morning Juxtaposed with the Profundity of the Garden of Eden, (or, Friday, October 4, 2013)	99
Love Me but Fear Me	100
Birds	102
Why?	103
Tiny Sparkles, Part 1	104
Away	105
To	107
The Mississippi Bridge	108
Falling for You, O American Continent in Drag	110
Gone	113
Tiny Sparkles, Part 2	115
It	116
I Am Going to Do This	118
Sometimes	119

Joy	121
Appreciating the Arts	123
Effortlessness Is a Love Poem in Disguise as Fuckery	124
Coffee Cup	127
True	129
Starlight	130
Cup	132
Sherry	133
Recipes for Happiness	135
Orange	136
My Own	137

Book I

The End of the Rose

Symbiosis

> *"...and the road was always hungry."*
>
> —Ben Okri

Nothing grounds you at the beginning

Of a journey. Starbucks

Is an anchorless sea. Bulletin boards

Above black tables with cookie crumbs

Advertise churches and bands.

Move me a mountain. Move me towards the sea.

When I open my eyes, I haven't even written

A love poem. You are not a country, but several.

Box of the heart, long novel I haven't written.

Or a castle in a cloud. Long song on the music of night.

An intricate jewel box of the imagination. I care, now,

About this history of living with my eyes closed.

Almost Finished

The history of living with one's eyes closed is mine.

The future is the hope that one will live with open eyes.

I do not even know what this is.

Chrysanthemums, I adore the river of that word,

Chrysanthemums, red roses, white roses.

How the light flows into me. *Daffodils.*

What is it that I have not wanted to see?

Necklace

I am a pain in the neck, and I must own

My pain-in-the-neck-ness. This is tough,

But denial gets you nowhere but some stupid thing.

Blue fire is what I'm after, what you have,

What you forgive in me, what you remembered.

Wine bottle's end, where the dregs

Mix with dust mites (if you leave the bottle

In the bedroom corner, where things go to be

Forgotten). Remember me into a blaze. Talk to me.

Loneliness was a red brick street,

But the sparrows always came and populated it,

And made me smile, despite the fact I never gave

Them crumbs. Look at me now.

Look at me with your dark eyes.

In the darkness of your light there are angels.

Gold is our color. Silver is the air we move through.

Made of Light

The world careens on the axis of a pop song

Made of light. The air resonates with its many

Facets. Reality has dimensions, they say.

What exists, and what doesn't? The most interesting

Things do not even exist. All of existence

Is the shadow of what doesn't exist.

Words on billboards are thresholds.

And doorways open into what is mostly lies.

Your doctor might be out to get you,

But you still need medicine, Jessica.

Winter Music and Musing on Summer in L.A.

You were a scarlet-painted door for me

With brass, dear Heather. You moved through time

As if it were a whirlpool, and you had a glass

Of champagne in your hand. It's a glass house

Of a world for some people, but some people

In glass houses are immune to stones.

You wrote all the koans. Your heart was a riddle.

Your champagne bubbled obnoxiously.

Superstar

It was wonderful to feel weak and \

Vulnerable around you.

You moved through late evening sunsets

As if it was all California.

The end of the movie was always

In sight for you, but never happened.

The camera of spacetime just kept

Rolling, and you had your paparazzi

Under control, as if they were Doberman

Pinschers eating biscuits from your milky hand.

You picked walnuts and cracked them with your fists.

End

It's winter inside me

And you're a thousand miles

And summers away in L.A.

It's so cold outside.

I zip up the rain,

Then head outside to take the subway.

My skull is a basketball.

Part of my heart is the world.

I wait by the train tracks,

Thinking of a better time

When the sparrows loved me.

And I did their bidding

When they told me to keep my strength.

Having nothing else to tell me this,

I did.

Loss and Resurrection

for M.

There is a wound somewhere.

Somewhere is everywhere when I think of you,

And you slip out of my pocket

Like a lucky penny.

And now I resurface

In the pop of your echoing bubblegum.

Younger one, I admire you.

Don't look up to me so much.

I am just a monster playing a fiddle.

My wings are all in tatters like rags,

But then again, that's why I think you like me.

I go around acting all holy or something.

This is precisely why I like you, too.

Wound

I was in a phase

Where I wished I had wings.

Because, you see, I needed them.

In the Beverly Center, they almost appeared,

And for a moment I felt them sparkling,

Like a new purse from an expensive store

Like The Limited or Gucci.

Paris sometimes comes to you.

Some cities can't stay still.

They disappear and reappear, repeat,

renew their own codas.

Shhhh. Few know this.

Wings

The impromptu gold glitter of suddenly

Halleluiah

My love, slip through me again

Send me a letter

Send myself back to me

Let me see you

Caring

Let me care

It's called opening

What has been forever sealed

Up until now

In its own flight

Walking On Clouds

for Misha

1.

Fairy tales are for the future

Parts of us who will need to be loved.

The world's version of love

Is better than heaven's, but don't tell

Anyone this. It's no fun being dead.

We must keep our brilliance, sharing it.

Yet we must keep up illusions.

If we thought this world was it,

That would be too banal,

Or maybe it would be heaven.

Do you understand?

2.

In my dreams I fly flags of imaginary

Countries ruled by imaginary philosopher kings

Who have been put together by other thinkers

As puzzle pieces. Whatever. If the pieces fit too well,

I don't fly the flag.

3.

Dream me a rainbow, love,

And tie my hands with it,

And never let me go.

Sun

for Misha

The sun is a river tied around dark bedposts.

I am talking about both memory and hope.

I don't like freedom except when I kill it.

Own me. Make me yours. Lightweight chaos

Is fun, and it's a great beginning. Thanks

For ignoring my ugliness. I have never

Been so flattered in my life. I am Medusa

And Jesus both. It's a weird combination,

I know. Sometimes thoughts when I think

Them, while looking at the light in the trees,

Are airborne. Ambient visions get the party

Going. And the world is nothing and everything

That ever was.

Nothing

Do you know what you are doing?

I ask myself. And you are nothing if

The word "if" isn't a hole in your sweater.

Wear holes in your clothes.

It's a day that smells of yard, yarn, coffee,

Peaches and dark wool, cotton balls,

And cigarettes, and I am making a poem

Out of it. Rising slowly after cleansing

Dreams that were water and fire.

Lavender. Ice-blue. Blue fire. A rumpled

Bedspread covered in flower patterns.

You are nothing if your sleep isn't whole.

You are a hole in my sleep and I pass through it

Into heaven, then fall to Earth again before waking.

I must keep on waking and waking and waking.

My Taste in Men

Taste the end of my rose in cold black water.

It's *The Book of the Dead,* where the water

Is sleep by the shore of some old neighborhood

Where God lived, still lives, will continue

On living forever.

Glenn Gould is humming

Patterns of snowfall, gentlest one, glitter.

An off-key bell at the North

Pole listens for the notes to play.

Love is everything and translations are useless.

Don't accept love that is nothing.

Wait until it's all, and wait until it's ripe,

And even if it's cold outside,

And we're both shivering, let God bless our winter.

Remembering the Dawns of Yesteryear, Waking up Today at 10:36 A.M.

Hit the white notes and translate the voice of Juno

Into water. Take the scratchy feathers and make them

Soap bubbles in autumn on the piano's black keys.

Bring Medieval Latin in. The *Carmina Burana*

Is great to listen to at night when one has mania, I know.

A swarm of bees in the brain effervesces,

Red as the blood in an original Artemesia

Gentilesci painting. Bleed. Breathe.

Wash up in the river, and if there is no river,

Use the rain.

Dawn

for Gillian

I remember when we walked

Home from the place of your employment,

St. Viateur Bagel, in the dead of January.

It was dawn at the *Super déjeuner* place,

And we had sides of tomato slices, hash browns,

And *fèves au lard.* That was dawn.

What else could dawn ever be?

January Sun

The sun is a giant January orange, snug

In a cloud's palm, turning the city to crisp leaves.

The coals of the sun pop on the ground, hissing.

God love Montreal's skyline to the north,

Where it's all a maze of brutalist architecture.

As the blue is born out of darkness,

The night evaporates like foam.

We loved each other there, dear friend,

In the city where one's pink wool mittens

Were worth their weight in gold in fairytales.

Limbs

I'm in suburban Washington, now,

Back from my long journey without luggage.

The limbs of trees outside the picture-sized

Window show me branches laden with

Red birds and black peaches.

I drink coffee (insert profound banality here,

Like continuing to breathe), and I read as I stare

Out the window. Pink figs and mauve grapes.

I read physics. Starlight appears.

Travel the textbooks based on Einsteinian

Visions, and you get the rhythm, no, I am lying.

I, compulsive liar, daydreaming about you,

Also a daydreamer.

Follow me. You'll get nowhere, and it's the best place.

The center here in this poem is the center of everything.

Light

A picture window gleams.

Temperature of ice in tantrics of crystals.

I see the sun and the water.

It's Maryland light.

O most durable band-aid for a broken heart,

Why do you manifest on Earth in the form of ice cream

In a small handmade bowl?

In January, there could be better things. The idea.

The idea of something, anyway, would be good, now.

The thought of hugging teddy bears repulses me

Like hornets' nests. I need the catharsis of bleed,

Bleed, bleed.

Heal, bleed, heal and scar yourself

With the *Carmina*

Burana taking off on white wings. Jessica, I think you

Have that on CD.

Wheel

A bleeding heart is like a wheel that keeps turning

As we are turning. I'm turning slowly into gladiolas

In a vase in February. Into the silence

Of the birds, I turn. Bird of birdsong, green

And maroon thrum.

Do you want

A cup of daffodil, a wineglass of gold? That's it?

The world is turning, and like sands in an hourglass,

These are the days of our lives.

Two for a dollar.

A petal falls from a white lily in a vase

Veined with lipstick

Pink, and wilts on the mahogany dining room table,

Next to a fork and knife, both stainless steel,

And the color of the sky out the window.

Lares and Penates

The Penates and Lares in this house live in the coffee

Maker. They chortle as the machine

Percolates its last drop. Thank-you, Folgers in my cup.

The world is bleeding into it, and Jessica,

You know your

    evil. Now, learn your bright diamond of

        goodness.

The Sun Is Going Down

The world bending into it. There is no going back.

The color gold always moves forwards,

From black to purple to pink to yellow to gold to blue

To black. Around and around it goes, this wheel.

Coda.

The world bending into it. There is no going back.

The color gold always moves forwards,

From black to purple to pink to yellow to gold to blue

To black. Around and around it goes, this wheel.

Coda.

There Is No Going Back

for Heather

Butterscotch cake in the shape of lips

With pink frosting

Is what you handed out for free.

In Paris, in front of the Coco Channel Boutique, you—

Aced your own act.

You gave people cake to prove a point

I still can't figure out.

You came back to Montreal

With a Parisian accent.

We shopped for bread,

Among the stalls in Atwater Market

You pronounced oregano "Ronald Oregano"

And Bay leaves, "The Bay Leaves Much to Be Desired."

There is always much to be desired,

Like the way you said, "Lily

Like "euly," that flower's true name. Each "eu" a shape

Of a flower petal, your lips and eye-sparkles.

We went out on the town to Boulevard St-Laurent

Where they served popcorn in wicker baskets

In pool shark bars. We said, "Euly"

To each other, and grinned maniacally.

Blue Fire

We began mincing everything

Like ballerinas. We were even a little mean

To each other. You kept losing your wallet,

Bitch. It was fun. So this is what people mean

When they say they dream of what it was like back

In the day? Back then, we could shove to the front

Of any crowd without saying "Excuse me."

We had so much confidence, then,

In the world, and in ourselves,

But not so much in each other.

I get really nostalgic about it, sometimes.

It was the way we applied lipstick

Like the word "euly" to our lips. Why not?

Why not say it was that?

The Fire Tree

In winter, in the morning, when we were not partying,

We'd sit in the park near your house.

There was always that one tree whose leaves

Turned fire-red in autumn, and kept its leaves on

Like icy fire

In winter. In the whitest snow

In the park, there we would be,

Two *Blanche-Neiges,* as the Haitian men called

Out to us on St. Joseph Boulevard,

And this red tree the color of fire

Blazing between us.

That was something like love

We had between each other.

Self-Deception

Well, as the band Modest Mouse says

In one of their songs,

"I've worked really hard to be the ass that I am."

Smoking a cigarette in the rain,

I cannot stop thinking about thinking,

Just about googling the past,

Which is, in many ways, the present.

Present this scenario to me:

Three coffee cups on a cluttered table,

One cup made out of paper, two mugs

Full of cigarette butts.

Reality is reality, and it will always be.

I don't have to accept it or like it, but I'll accept it.

Not far away from this scene, Act I bleeds into Act II,

And, I, a house, am a high-ceilinged house,

And in my yard there is a pruned

Pear tree. Walk out of me and wait

By the bus stop, near the tree as high as a wall,

And listen to the branches quake, loaded

With birds.

Baguette

Fuck Oedipus Rex.

We always knew him Biblically.

We're sapphire-girls

And we knew it as walked through Atwater Market

Shopping for Baguette.

We knew we were ripe as pure apples

In the form of oranges.

Our clothes fit us like that.

We wore them that way, too.

The Clothes We Wore

With holes in them

As were jeans not a kiss, skirts sometimes

Plaid like Montreal sunsets with spring clouds

Red jeans

Denim you said was just the color of the sky

Really early in the Arizona evening

I said Montreal is nothing like Phoenix

It just simmers but never burns down

And it's not New York

Or Boston green-blue-gray

Montreal's ether spills like maroon wine

We went everywhere the sunset was

Overflowing as we touched

Hands

Walking through Atwater Market,

One is reminded of the olden days,

Because the brick is water-stained.

Even the pigeons are made of light.

Shopping for baguette, I feel so unique.

The blue absent in everything makes it all feel

Like nothing's as far away as the sky.

God is both antique, and the sign of the future

Flying like a bird towards you.

To the left is a woman selling tomatoes

Who looks a little like a cabbage.

Her face is perhaps also like bread.

This woman you know

Is not like you, Jessica. She knows the mysteries

Of both work and love.

Each Other

for Misha

Since the day we were born, I cried for you.

This might be bullshit or it might be the truth.

You choose. Pepper tree, Georgia magnolia,

Looking for baguette and brie in a farmer's market

In South Carolina, and finding them all at one kiosk

Is a little like Heaven, but more wonderful,

Because it's impromptu is out of place.

I like things like that. Out of whack but in whack

With the universe.

Finding the world, stumbling into love

When you least expect it. Wait.

Don't wait. Walk. Don't walk.

Obey all traffic signals. Listen

To what God says. I am trickling

Into a coffee cup.

I am avoiding all grocery stores

This morning

That will send me reeling

Into epileptic seizures

With overpowering halogen

Ceiling lighting.

Thinking of you, I avert my eyes.

I smoke a cigarette, and it's stale,

And still I love the world,

Because you're you.

You

The world is a diamond on fire.

Can I say, "I love you"

And have that be a joke,

Or not be a joke,

Because I love you so much,

It's kind of

But not really

Even funny?

Hats! Scarves! Mittens!

You make me barf with rapture,

Seizing lions by the horns.

Fight me

Don't fight the sun

Kiss the stars

And their awkward light, their blazing starwork!

Rapture

Works on us backwards and forwards.

And rapture is a crazy rupture,

But there is nothing to do but be practical about it

If possible, and make a list of poems

I am going to read aloud,

After I get paid and go to the corner store to buy milk.

I am going to read aloud,

If possible, and make a list of poems

But there is nothing to do but be practical about it

And rapture is a crazy rupture,

Works on us backwards and forwards.

Earth

for Misha

Suddenly, I'm on planet Earth.
Here, be with me. Tingle up and down my spine.
Roll me in butter and poppy seeds then fry me
Like the Ancient Romans did to dormice.

Be a little creepy with me in a garden of Eden
Zoo where peacocks fan like feathery spider webs.
Feats of circus acts and fire swallowing may be real.

Blow me a kiss. Why ask me why I have written
This poem? These days everything I do seems
Super-motivated by my thoughts of you. You dream!
You dream and you make me dream, too!

For You

And I want you, despite the fact

That I must accept a reality I dislike.

Reality demands that we accept it,

Though I don't have to like it. As Slavoj Žižek

Says, "I don't like reality.

Who says I need to like it? Reality

Is stupid." Yet I am stupider.

Reality went to Yale. The trees are still

For us, flirting with the autumn morning.

Don't get so technical about it, I tell myself.

Shhhh. Can't you hear the whole planet

Listening as if I were whispering, not shouting

What I have to share?

A Short Poem about Being Here

With every crunch of baguette,

I wish I were here. I am! Ha, ha!

Lion

Iron curlicues of café terraces

Ache when it rains

And the coffee is nearly hot.

Chicago.

This is what it's like to read Paris

Vogue and think backwards to the Midwest.

In time, Montreal will appear to you.

Popcorn in a wicker basket in a pool shark bar,

Rufus Wainwright on the radio, Halleluiah.

The waitress gived out free drinks to the regulars.

I love waiting on the other end of blue.

I love you here, and I love you there.

Come, lion-tamer,

And crack your whip, and make me bow down

To the ground you walk on.

Rain

In that rain, I shove nonchalantly

Through a crowd,

Munching baguette.

Crows hide in the bushes,

Their peek-a-boo eyes of gold shining.

As if we had a care in the world

For anything but them and their messenger silence,

I know, you don't have to tell me with an eye-roll.

As if we were not in love, then in love,

Then not in love, then not, then, then. Again!

That's love.

As if we had a care for any of this sweetness.

Book II

Time Went on and the Future Passed Judgment

For Julia

I know something. I wanted to say I

Was gone before I even tried out winter.

It went something

Like this, "Thank-you, Julia, for believing in me."

I don't mean to be a downer, but without her

Summer was a bird caged in a Quaalude.

She taught me how to get down and teach myself things,

Things one needed to know to stay above sea level.

In a TV commercial, the light was slanting just so.

"Get a little weirder to be good," she said.

"Standardized things keep the status quo. Fidget more."

So I put the calculus into God, and began

Teaching others how to win chess games,

Just by looking at the diagonals on the board,
Though I myself always lost to myself when I played.

The horizontal lines are easy, but it's the diagonals
That make the bishops spring
Up like stained glass flowers,

And bring a bit of a Cathedral's voice
Into it. We need to get holy
And nearly mystical about the game.

"Beg," she said with her eyes. "Learn to beg for
Everything. Respect everything you beg for and get."

Patricia

1.

I recently reached you by facebook message.//
Has it been that long? A lot has happened

In the past. A universe was born. Patricia,//
He knows my heart is the Garden of Eden.

Patricia, it is sunny today. What else can I say?//
Thank-you for teaching

Me that I had a poem in me, one I could write//
Over and over again.

2.//
Subtle variation

Is tantamount. A world came into being.

3.

It was like his heartbeat,

With the sun

Shining through the trees, pure and waving.

4.

It is his influence on birds that makes me happy.

Those birds have never before

Sung to me after dark, but yesterday, yesterday,

Yesterday.

5.

It has been fourteen hours and fifty-eight

Minutes since yesterday, and I drank coffee,

Smoked, relaxed, and bought scratch tickets today.

Lost some, won some, came out ahead, then halved

Like an apple sliced once.

I like my men thin and beautiful,

Smart, funny. They can make me feel free

While also making me feel

As if I also belong in a nice cool headlock.

Patricia, I like it this way. I think you think that's odd,

But you respect me being me.

I'm a big fan of love and the grip, you know.

I wear my hair up, these days.

It suits me just fine.

Patricia, I am his.

Arnold

"I'll be back," as they say. Time is a snake,

A road, a bazooka, a piece of gum we chew,

Eschew, get stuck to our left shoe. Space is an urban

Myth, a rowboat, a masterpiece waiting to happen.

Everything's a fucking poem if you leave it be

And don't slice it in half. The Terminator,

Too, knows this.

Act I

I have been playing my part as an actress

Playing an actress in her real life, again. Oh, my!

I have been hamming it up, laughing, having

Some fun. If you want to win at what you want

To win at, don't even play the game.

Go to the lions and make them tame,

Then play a round robin of baseball in your head

And steal your own mind back from advertisements.

It's time for some more coffee.

Who cares?

The One

for a guy I saw once

Is it so delusional of me to make up the notion

That the one who played pool as the light

Spun the air with dragon tattoos

Was the one. I leaned up against the mahogany bar.

I was complete with cigarette holder and brown tweed.

I think I am dreaming myself, again,

Against all improbabilities,

And in the light, there is hardly any room for you,

Unless you're capable of blowing open

The galaxy, which you are,

Which you have done, just now in this poem,

And I am now a house with green shutters.

The windows blow open.

Curtains dance.

The night will come again,

And all my ghosts from pool halls vanishing in trance

Music will come to haunt me, and once again

I'll feel so self-conscious here, and I'll just stand there

In the past, smoking a cigarette.

One

Who could save me but his eyes?

Earth-fire, the heavens blazing

So beautiful it's blasphemy,

And I am calm, and I am hyper,

And I am radioactive.

I am so happy that when I buy something

From a friend, I haggle up, not down.

Face the Music, Bitch

Well, you know,

I always was a bit of a bitch.

Ya mam suca. So?

What were we talking about, anyway?

Oh my god. Oh, yes, the day

I thought there was no hope,

But still felt

It tingling in my right knee,

In the tree with the birds in it,

My left knee shivers whenever it's going to rain,

And I felt the birds

And around the edges of the air,

Just now.

And this is what love is kind of like.

Book III

Subito Cogito, Ergo Sum

Shine

Like godstuff. Always.

A lot has happened to me.

I worked, played, got drunk, got sober,

Smoked, stared, cried so quietly that only the birds

Could hear me. Crickets and coffee mugs.

As I was saying, a lot has happened

Over the past ten years. But I never lost my wings,

Just lost it, wrote a symphony with the help

Of only my intuition and a ballpoint pen,

Then lost that, too. Only with scrap

Paper siphoned from this world, along with all out left

Socks that get mysteriously lost in the dryer, I accepted

The hum, the thrum.

And I have always been able to access

The wrong part of my mind.

We know what you're up to, universe.

We're not as stupid as we look, though sometimes

We are.

But never underestimate carbon-based life-forms.

That is my lesson for today.

Define yourself.

The sky is blue.

Define yourself. Don't let others do it for you.

The sky is not a glass paperweight.

I am not a piece of scrawled-on paper

About to blow away.

Are we writing

Poetry, yet? Wherever is there

To arrive? Patterns. P.S. Love like there is no end

To love, and never ask at the wrong

Moment, "Is there a cheese platter

At the end of all this?"

Corona

As I uprooted weeds on the farm,

I made a hole in the ground

Where I could balance a bottle

Of Corona. At the end of that August,

I would be diagnosed with psychosis

N.O.S., not otherwise specified.

It's a little secret, so please don't tell anyone.

The thorns brushed my hands,

But I did not get scratched.

I listened to Nick Drake on vinyl and felt old,

In my living room at dawn, at twenty-four,

Smoking, thinking, thinking about nothing.

I still tasted the lime, even these days,

Stuck on the lip of my Corona bottle,

As it was back then, soggy with sun.

It was what made me

Happiest, then.

No

What is there to do

But walk the gangplank

Into the moment, which is always a squall?

In the second half of the day

That was my thirty-eighth birthday,

I was sitting in a café

On a cool, sunny afternoon,

At 12:19. I never did

Get what I meant

Before this.

Heartbeat

It can take over a room, sometimes.

Like a stopwatch, like a race,

Like something existential

That has no name

But is a lot like no other ether, either.

The end can be felt like a song

Coming to an end, but there is the replay

Button, so don't worry. Guitar riffs,

Face cream, cheap cherry-colored plastic

Jewelry. The whole shebang.

A cup of coffee at 3:23 in the afternoon.

I am old and I am in love and I love it,

And I love myself, and I love you,

And now I need to listen,

Listening to heartbeats in the leaves.

Morning

Me and my Dad were coming back to Las Vegas,

Where slot machines mocked us like possessed robots.

We dealt with it by eating Fruit Loops.

What there was

Is not what there is. Dad's in a hospital, now,

But in Vegas back in the day,

We saw a UFO in the Nevada Desert.

It looked like an amusement park ride.

And out of respect for my elders,

I never bring up the UFO sighting.

My Dad doesn't like weird stuff,

Or, not too weird, anyway. Even me, I'm a little bit

Too far off the cliff for him, as if I were not merely

On the edge, but as if I had already jumped off,

And knew how to fly.

Working a Day Job in Boston, Massachusetts

I like going into the office at midnight.

My office is a laboratory, and I make my own hours.

The world is always morning to me,

Even at midnight, especially at midnight.

Maybe the whole world is midnight

Turning its pitch daffodil face towards

Morning. The petals say, hello, gold,

Hello-red-cold-gold

As well as blue-tinted darkness, a silver like it's black.

Midnight is like that, a cusp

With several colors clashing

And chasing each other.

I could bake cookies today.

I could ponder the ether. Or you.

Edible. You are so edible.

Don't wear the colors of midnight

With other colors of midnight,

Unless you're going to the office,

Where a little tackily over-matched is okay.

I never understood

Why beige went with beige.

I am proud of my office job, O you.

I am proud I am a worker bee in a laboratory-office.

I never understood

Why American-born women

Make themselves a little ugly

For work. Never be a two-by-four,

Loves, unless you're going bowling.

Then, I can see that tactic's practical reality.

But I'm midnight on the other side

Of the world, today, O women in my office.

When you're getting

A sandwich in the building's cafeteria,

Think of me a lot like a vicious but beautiful songbird.

Café Café

for my father, William Richards Harman

After seeing that the Thunderbird Café

Had dishwater for cappuccino, Dad,

We went in search of the Café Café.

We found it on Dysart Road, near a Kinko's.

The place was predominantly green,

And was partly Eden, partly Jungle,

And half the inside of the Coliseum.

Once you were metaphysically back in Rome,

I could ask, "What is your territory?"

You loved Italy, and I, *Lac Caché*

Up north where once I went camping with my aunt,

Near the Boreal. A Canadian daughter

Is the price you pay for draft dodging.

No Disney communion for me, no Hollywood,

Just porn in a cul-de-sac in a Montreal ghetto.

The English there go crazy. They don't do so well

In isolation, left to feed off each other.

Even they know to never say, "Voulez-vous

Dansez avec moi," your one French phrase.

The Anglo Montrealers

Watch movies and walk their dogs, big

Chows with sad crows' eyes. It's so easy

To love, so easy to hate. I love-hate many

People. You're okay, Dad, so love-hateable

Within the swirl of my cappuccino.

I stir, adding some more sugar, then stirring again,

Take a little sip.

Why not remember you as beautiful?

Silencia

You said things and sometimes did not say things,

Yes or no being always already irrelevant,

As you always let me sip cappuccino

In any long pause.

You could look

At my lip-shape, but just so that you could begin

To finally understand what silence was.

Daddy

Thank-you for Rome, Montreal, and Phoenix, Arizona.

Why not? Why not say we're both two countries,

Seven stars, never the same, drifting, now staying still.

Let the ripples sway out from here.

We've come to rest and know solace.

Me, in Boston, and you,

In Queens, New York. I'll write you.

I'll send the letter. Thanks for making me.

It's a great feeling to have been conceived,.

Jessica, I ask myself now, how did the facts affect you?

Hole in One

Arizona was always not Rome to you,

Not Montreal to me, so what was it?

Bagels, sand, radioactive sunsets.

An orange or two or three.

Some skyscrapers where no one ever seemed

To be working. Lightning in a purple grapefruit grove.

Soft rain mixing

With evening sprinklers.

Sudden silence around weeping willows

Above man-made ponds. Everything

A golf-course maze of mist, it seemed, unreal.

Jessica, the desert stars are coming out for you.

Being Denim the Color of the Sky—Say What?!

That was years ago,

And I've faded, now.

I keep shape-shifting, but that's the part of me

That's still not in America, that never arrived.

The day before yesterday, I thought I was a mistake.

Was it a mistake to come here, and let Montreal ice

Melt to candle-light? Everything is difficult.

Even love.

I cannot explain this, unless you know.

Soggy Cornflake Morning Juxtaposed with the Profundity of the Garden of Eden, (or, Friday, October 4, 2013)

I wonder things that only

Half have words,

Then I eat soggy cornflakes. These are happy

Mornings, these days.

You're not here, because my roommates

Unleashed their venom upon you,

But Babycakes—

It was just venom on top of ice cream,

With a cherry

On top.

Don't fear the cherry. It's just a cherry.

Love Me but Fear Me

I want you in inverse proportion

To how I want the world. I don't want the world.

I control it,

Anyway. I don't want to control you

But I would

Control you if I didn't already

Know that my heart is freedom. My heart is Eden.

There are blue-green pears, red

Apples, and black

Birds with emerald eyes

Singing there. They sing for you.

Their song is about peaches, mittens, psalms, codes

For secrets too secret to be

Secret, so are things

Anyone could know if they tried.

Birds

Sometimes they even sing at night before I fall

Asleep. Last night, they did.

I was once in love with Satan, but, Saint Francis,

You are so much sweeter. You make any day great,

Even if I don't start it out with breakfast cereal

But start it out instead with coffee and cigarettes.

In poems,

Just for the sake of writing a poem,

I'll put a reference to an unwritten poem,

One which is, but is never written.

Because that's where I was

Before I found you. It is where I am going,

Where we are all going,

And it is not my poem, and that is why I can't write it,

Only write about it. Love has nothing to do with this.

Why?

Thank-you to all who have listened and turned away.

Tiny Sparkles, Part 1

for Rick, in memoriam, 1956 - 2012

And there you Making tiny shadows out of cold sparkles.

There was nothing at that moment to say.

There you were in the snow,

At the bus stop, drinking a Coke,

And the snow was gently falling.

Away

Yet, there is away a "yet" when we decide to keep

Going. I've weather storms without dorms,

And with dorms, too. I've packed them all

In a knapsack and taken a bus halfway across America.

Minneapolis, Minnesota, to Montreal, Quebec,

Is a long way to travel without a coffee cup.

I've danced

On a street corner in Hoboken, New Jersey.

I went around the block a few times, and caught

A roof on fire. Jessica, look at yourself in the mirror.

Ask yourself, "Who are you?"

To

To be more than this, you said.

And to know it. To know the meaning of it.

To have once been an ounce of sunlight

In a Ziploc bag in the shape

Of a blonde girl. *"La plus belle fille au monde,"*

A stranger said to the sidewalk the color

Of a five o'clock shadow as he passed me.

The most beautiful suicide is no suicide at all.

I drank Satanic coffee, lived to love again,

To say, "Hello." A figure eight carved in the sand,

In another language is called, *thamania,*

Waiting for the tide to erase it.

And for me to draw it once again, clearly, this time,

As clear as infinity in any tongue.

The Mississippi Bridge

In the Midwest, you said, people don't get emotional

About anything, not even rebuilding their houses

After tornadoes. So I went there, to see, and found

Myself penniless in Minnesota. I wandered

Over the Mississippi Bridge, then the Wabasha,

Made of American flags in the wind.

Flapping on the parapets and watching the cargo

Ships skim the sunny surface of the water, I felt vertigo,

Knowing something was over. This falling through you,

And through myself, too—I had come to the edge

Of the river, and did not jump, but walked

All the way across. After the bridge.

Ohio Street wound upwards,

Zigzagging up a mountain,

Then beyond, to a place where people lived

In modest but comfortable houses,

And did not fear the cold of the night.

Falling for You, O American Continent in Drag

And I didn't tell you I fell again and again.

Crawling out of the muck in Montreal,

I found myself face to face with a mannequin

In a second-hand clothing shop.

Her painted eyes made glitz seem like the silver-black

Belly of an eel. If the sky didn't say it first,

Didn't want

Me to have shock therapy or move in that direction,

Maybe it would have

Happened, or been a little different. I loved the world

Though, and I still love it and I fear it. Fearing love

Is a healthy thing—or not? Ask the glitzy

Ones in Café Cafeteria, on *Boulevard St. Laurent.*

They listen to the right music.

And the coolest of the Montreal hipsters

Read only when absolutely necessary,

Same getting tattoos, say, of a snake

On one's shaved skull.

They know protocol. It's all terrifying.

Poetic *duende* cannot be a crutch

Except when dancing on street corners in New Jersey,

Smiling and standing still when cop cars roll by.

Tell me, Jessica, should America be

Socialist, Communist, or Capitalist? I don't know.

Go ask the starlets in Hollywood.

Let someone else besides me decide,

As long as there is love.

Gone

And I was broken into being and into being humanly

Compassionate. Abdel let me stay in the rooming house

For free, as long as I eventually gave him back the key.

I found myself there, in acceptance rather than ego,

In the youth hostel, where the sheets were striped,

The comforters polka-dotted, and each of the four

Walls painted a different color. Yellow, blue,

Orange, pink. In the middle of the room

Was a Corinthian pillar, wood painted white.

I was a curlicue there, for an evening. No, I was not:

I was not the curlicue on the column, but it was the map

For my imagination. I dreamed the future, there.

The earth can be transparent, sometimes,

But the concrete things in that hotel made the universe

Opaque, again. So, I took a shower, and went out to flirt

In a café on Saturday night, and it felt okay,

A lot like falling, or traveling once again

Without luggage.

Tiny Sparkles, Part 2

It's periwinkle beneath our boot heels. It really is.

The world is only half of a solid substance.

At high noon, I effervesce.

A city is lonely and then happy among the spin

Of its own seasons. You give me topspin, Baby.

You give me gravity, and thought. Still, I sparkle,

Lightweight in your stillness

When the breeze that you are pauses

Is something happening.

You listen to many things this way.

I listen to you, listening.

It

How beautiful the snow really is.

It's a bird in flight. It's a bird sitting still

On the left edge of a balcony at the end of Cannaught

Street. You can read minds. A hush of snowfall

So luminous it's blue. I can't wait for January.

I love men in winter coats and mittens,

Shirts open at the neckline.

It's a rough journey,

Even a tougher one to get out of here.

It is not a prison,

This, though it's cold. It's warm, too.

This sinking, tickling, trick of floating

On the sea's foam. Float. We are buoyant from time

To time, and we know it.

I Am Going to Do This

It is morning and I am thinking of you,

Bedridden in New York, eating that hospital food.

I wonder every day how you are,

Though often I say nothing, and let the silence fly

Across a continent, and fill whatever it is

That needs filling, the joy, that needs how I do this,

And how I want to do this. A poem

Is nothing but dark-space.

Or is a poem a photon?

Sometimes, things are dual,

Like the universe of positive and negative forces.

Love, light, no light at all sometimes.

Sometimes

In the bungalow where my grandparents lived,

There were always knickknacks

And hints of art, even, among the Davenports.

A watermill in oil above the candy dish. An original

Picasso print on the lime green walls, showing two

People hugging. The smell of dolls made out of apple

Leather,. Ah, the melon cleanser and lemon pepper.

There were no sestinas between me

And my grandmother, just advertisements for breakfast

Cereal, just donuts, trips to T.J. Maxx., and burgers

At Claim Jumper. I bought

Gold sequins, and impressed Grammy.

There is no whisper in my ear since she died.

Joy

Let me tell you a story, using only glass

Shards, a rubber band, an earring, and a banana.

Let it be funny, but not a joke.

It will be like a McGuyver

Episode. In solitary confinement, just breathe.

All I have in my mind is a pen

And a chocolate bar, can I escape?

Can I escape myself if I remember

Many positive events in the past? I am so cool.

I'm like that when I feel your iridescent joy.

You make me such a better person,

And not in a clichéd way. You make me less McGuyver,

More chess, more joke, less cigarettes, more sweetness

But less sugar in my coffee. I love you.

Appreciating the Arts

All I have now is a root beer candy, a doily, and a pen.

How do I get out of here, and enter the spirit

Of the universal mysteries? Shakespeare

Could do it with an autumn leaf and a strand of hair,

Picasso with three or four shades of blue.

Rembrandt, an eye that held the glow of a wing

In light. Leonardo? A path winding in the distance

Beyond a smile that essentially told

All the world to please go and screw itself.

Mona Lisa, I love your sassy charm. Jessica, be more

Like her.

Effortlessness Is a Love Poem in Disguise as Fuckery

> *"Black milk of daybreak, we drink you at night, we drink you at morning, we drink and we drink"*
>
> –Paul Célan

> *"Powdered water: what would you add?"*
>
> —Steven Wright

I am going to tell you a story with black milk

And a penny thrown into a wishing well.

I am going to make dazzle cake

Out of powdered water.

I am going to find out where poetry gains its crux to spin

Around and then remain still and sink in.

I am going out to find an argument

And lose it to make someone feel better about analysis.

I am going to find a cute omen of a raven or a crow

At a café. I am. I mean to convince you, not deceive you.

I have a way of getting confused by all poetry.

Should it be a process of clarification

That does not eschew the gods? Whatever.

I have my Kindle full of ebooks,

And an empty coffee cup that I am about to refill.

God. I like God. Yet I should love Him.

*

I just refilled my coffee cup. Now I am thinking of love,

Bongos, calico-patterned barrettes, nail

Polish, sugar, and you.

Coffee Cup

Coffee cups and holy grails are different things.

One is full of morning, the other, the evening

Of eternity. What is eternity? I have an idea

Of some beads to thread along a necklace.

Waves made of words, we bounce off and through

Each other. I have choices. I have nerve.

I have a handful of quotes and a manual

On how to read a silver heron as the bird

Blasts off the surface of a steel-colored river.

America, when will we rediscover you?

America, when will we discover you in the first place?

I have been born again at 12:52 at au bon pain,

Thinking of threading a loom and weaving

Together water and light.

True

Truth is one more layer of bullshit.

Sparrows hop here and there

By the train tracks, pecking at small crumbs,

Which are God's voice.

Which is the feast.

Starlight

Everyone's a genius all the time.

—Jack Kerouac

My scream got lost in a paper cup.

—Tori Amos

Light ties the universe together.

Tori Amos can do it with a pair of torn jeans

And a scream

Lost in a paper cup. Genius is a burden

Where every glimpse of light weighs a ton

On your back. You know it.

You know it and we all know it. Good.

Now, let's get to thinking about something else.

Let's all try for a moment to not be geniuses.

We will move in disguise.

Cup

Ha, ha! Truth serum cupcake, anyone?

I am happy. That's why I'm an idiot.

Sherry

Julia Child takes a sip of sherry

In the foreground of the egg timer

Ticking a background beat. A beat

In acting happens. If you have intuition,

You fear the angel food cake. If you have genius,

You fear the edges of cliffs, and a cliff

Can be any moment, anywhere. A frame

Of mind called the blue zone

And a rose in a bud vase in a café

Where all the tables are made of ghosts.

We know this but we don't know other things

Because we are the living.

Recipes for Happiness

Julia Child always had her Sherry on hand.

So what do we have? Flowers, roses, Phlox, daisies,

Tums, and the birds landing after they glide,

And begin to sing, looking at us with black

Diamonds that beg for crumbs

And glimpses into our world.

It must look so strange to them.

Orange

The book I show you receives the cold.

It receives a smile of welcome, this book, this cold.

I didn't say this.

I didn't say that.

I have so many words that I want to tell you

That are not my own.

I cannot say them.

My Own

I give them to you, these words.

The Word is always already here, there. Then, here.

It is more beautiful than many words.

Yet. It is merely an invisible variable,

Variation on itself producing more variations

On itself

And what it once was, and what it could be,

Will be, not yet, never, maybe, and it always says,

One thing, "Light" and "Yes."

Biography

Jessica Harman earned her B.A. in Creative Writing from Concordia University in Montreal. She was born and raised in Montreal, and moved to Boston in 2001. She has worked as a video store clerk, artist's assistant, editor, medical research assistant, and teacher. Her work has appeared in literary journals such as "Arion," "Bellevue Literary Review," "Nimrod," "Rosebud," "Spillway," "Stand," and "Tears in the Fence." Her first full-length collection of poetry, "Dream Catcher," was published by Aldrich Press in Palo Alto, California, in 2012. She currently lives in Massachusetts.

141